Everything You Need to Know About

TEEN MARRIAGE

A marriage will bring many changes. Teens who are aware of
and prepared for these changes will have a better chance for a
successful marriage.

Everything You Need to Know About
TEEN MARRIAGE

Eleanor H. Ayer

THE ROSEN PUBLISHING GROUP, INC.
NEW YORK

Published in 1990, 1997 by The Rosen Publishing Group, Inc.
29 East 21st Street, New York, New York 10010

Revised Edition 1997
Copyright 1990, 1997 by The Rosen Publishing Group, Inc.

Library of Congress Cataloging-in-Publication Data

Ayer, Eleanor H.
    Everything you need to know about teen marriage/Eleanor H. Ayer.
    (The need to know library)
    Includes bibliographical references and index.
    Summary: Examines the choices involved in teenage marriage, as well
as the joys, problems, expectations, and implications. Presents case studies
for and against teenage marriage.
    ISBN 0-8239-2502-1
    1. Teenage marriage—United States—Juvenile literature.
    [1. Marriage.]   I. Title. II. Series.
    HQ799.2.M3A94 1990
    306.81′0835—dc20   90-36553
                                              CIP
                                              AC

Manufactured in the United States of America.

Contents

Introduction

There are many reasons why you as a teen may begin to think about marriage. When you're in a romantic relationship with someone you really care about, it's only natural to start thinking about marriage. You enjoy spending time with this person, and you think maybe he or she is the one for you. You may be thinking how great it would be to live together and spend the rest of your life with that person.

Others may start thinking about marriage when there's a baby on the way. Some believe marriage will solve the problems in their lives.

Whatever your reasons for thinking about marriage, you need to understand that marriage means taking on a lot of responsibilities. Marriage is a partnership, like many relationships. When you have disagreements, you have to work them out with the other person. Remember that when you're married, you can't just walk away from an argument. You have to learn to compromise in order for your marriage to work.

This book will discuss the many aspects involved in a teen marriage, from finding the perfect mate to making the decision to marry. We will discuss the legal requirements teens need to meet before they can get married. We will explore how a baby will affect a teen marriage. And we will look at the different viewpoints about teen marriages. Should couples marry in their teen years, or should they wait until they are older?

Marriage will bring about a lot of changes. Your relationship has to be strong enough to endure those changes, good and bad, in order to last. The more you know about what's involved in a marriage, the better chance you'll have for a successful marriage.

In order to have a successful relationship, couples have to accept and love each other without trying to change each other.

Chapter 1

Finding the Right Person

Many of us fall into the trap of trying to find the perfect mate. But we learn after looking that no one is perfect. We all have flaws, so we have to keep that in mind when we're looking for the person we want to spend the rest of our lives with; he or she will have flaws too.

There are bound to be things about him or her that you may not like. The important thing is to not let those little differences ruin your relationship. By doing this, you accept and love that person without trying to change who he or she is. But it's also important to understand that if the differences are too great, and it isn't possible to resolve them, he or she may not be the right person for you.

How Well Do You Know Each Other?

Cheryl and Doug had been working together at the after-school program for two years. Doug admired and respected Cheryl's abilities with children.

Cheryl felt the same way about Doug. He was always on time and ready to work extra hours. It showed he had dedication and a sense of responsibility.

Sharing Common Values

Eventually, Cheryl and Doug started dating. They shared their feelings with each other on different topics, such as school, jobs, sex, drugs, children, and religion. They found that they had similar opinions and values in many areas.

Sharing the same values and opinions is a very important aspect in a relationship. Because they had similar values, it is less likely that Cheryl and Doug will face major problems caused by a difference of opinions. For example, Doug and Cheryl both believe two is the perfect number of children in a family. This will avoid problems later if they get married and are ready to start a family. On the other hand, if Cheryl doesn't want any children and Doug wants two, this can create problems for their marriage.

Compromise

However, this doesn't mean that you must find someone who agrees with everything you believe in. Also, if a couple doesn't agree on the number of children to have, it doesn't mean that they shouldn't get married. If two people truly love each other, they will compromise and try to work things out. Compromise involves the couple coming up with a decision that both can live with. The point is not that one will get what he or she wants and the other will be unhappy. Compromise means each person must give up a little of what he or she wants and make peace somewhere in the middle. For example, if Cheryl doesn't want any children, and Doug wants two, they may compromise and decide to have one child.

Friendship

Many couples also find that friendship is very important in a marriage. Very often, a husband's and wife's best friends are each other. Friendship and respect are the first steps in a strong marriage. Cheryl and Doug were good friends before they started dating. This means they were able to talk to each other and help each other with problems. Couples in a romantic relationship face different problems than those faced in a friendship. But if the couple is able to talk to each other, they have a better chance of working out their problems. Their friendship will help them face problems in their future together.

Respecting Each Other's Family and Friends

Our choice of friends reflects who we are. We like being with people who are similar to us, who do the same things and think the same way we do. Our friends understand and support us. They are important to us.

Likewise, our families are important to us. They are the people to whom we turn for guidance and help in times of need. They are the ones who have been with us all our lives.

Marriage doesn't mean leaving behind friends or family. In fact, it is just the opposite. When you decide to marry someone, you are accepting his or her friends and family as well. The person you love needs family and friends as much as he or she needs you.

Trusting Each Other

In a relationship, one of your greatest fears may be losing the person you love, possibly to someone else. If you let this fear go too far, it can turn into jealousy, which can ruin a relationship.

It is not unusual to feel as if you have to guard the person you love from others who you may think will take him or her away. But you have to remember that your loved one is not a piece of property. He or she chooses to be with you. You have to trust him or her to make the choice to stay with you. You have to have faith in yourself to

know that he or she cares about you enough not
to cheat on you.

For Better or for Worse

Marriage is a commitment to your partner. A
commitment is a promise that you will keep for a
very long time, no matter how hard it may be.
That is why you need to think long and hard
before you make a commitment to someone or
something.

On your wedding day, you promise to take your
partner "for better or for worse." What if some
things are "for worse?" What if money becomes a
problem? What if one of you is sick for a long
time? Are you sure that the kind of life you will
have with your partner will make you happy? You
need to answer questions like these honestly
before you make a commitment to marriage.

Chapter 2

Deciding to Marry

Making the decision to marry, at any age, can be difficult. You may be confused or uncertain. Many people may offer advice, but in the end, the decision is yours and that of your partner. As a teen, you may feel unprepared and afraid, but you are not alone.

Looking at the Facts
- More than 300,000 teens are married
- Eight out of every 100 female teens are married
- Two out of every 100 male teens are married

While 300,000 may seem like a lot of married teens, only half as many teens are getting married now as before 1950. During that time, marrying at a young age was normal. But today marrying young is often considered unwise.

Deciding to marry can be difficult at any age. You and your partner need to think about and discuss what's involved in a marriage before making any decision.

There are a lot of things to consider before you decide to get married. Make a list of questions and discuss them with your partner. Here are some things for both of you to think about:

- How will you support yourselves?
- Where are you going to live?
- Will one or both of you work?
- How will the chores be shared?
- Are you going to be able to finish school?
- If a baby is on the way, how will you cover the doctor and hospital bills, and who will take care of the baby once he or she is born?
- If a baby is not on the way, are you going to have children, and if so, when?
- Are you going to have time for each other after work, school, and taking care of the household?

Advice from Friends

It's a good idea sometimes to turn to friends for help. They may offer a point of view you haven't considered. They may give you helpful advice about whether you should or should not get married. No matter what anyone tells you, though, the final decision is yours.

Advice from Your Family

It's nice to be able to go to family for advice, but they may not want the same things you do.

Jack's girlfriend was pregnant, but they weren't ready to marry. "I didn't want to, and she didn't want to," said Jack. "Only my father wanted us to. I tried to tell him there were other choices. But all he did was slam the table and yell, 'You've got to do it. It's the honorable thing to do.'"

Nina told her mother that Mario had asked her to marry him. Her mother was very happy. "She started talking about being a grandmother, about fixing up our house. . . ." But Nina didn't want to hear those things. Now that Mario had really asked her, she wasn't at all sure she *did* want to get married. If only her mother would say no, that she was too young. That would be much easier than telling Mario she just wasn't ready to marry him.

Who Can You Talk to?

Everyone seems to know what you should do except you. What you really want is for someone to listen with an open mind. But who? There are such people. You'll find a list in the back of this book.

School counselors are trained to listen to and understand teens. They know that teen problems can be different than adult problems. They can help you sort out your own feelings. You can also speak to a religious leader, such as a minister or rabbi about problems. He or she will listen and try to help you.

Don't forget to talk to those who may know best—older people who *did* marry as teens. Did a teen marriage work out well for them? What do they have to say now, five or ten years later? What *advice* can they give you? Most of these people will be very glad to talk with you or listen to your worries.

Standing Up to Pressure

After you've talked to others, there are two more people you must listen to: yourself and your partner. You are the ones who must decide. There is often a lot of pressure involved in making big decisions. You can handle that pressure if you are honest with yourself. But you must be ready to say:

- My friends may think this is wrong, but it is my choice. I have to decide what is right or wrong for me.
- I may look at things differently when I am older. Right now I may not agree with what adults are telling me. But I will try to listen with an open mind, so I can make the right decision.
- I have faith in myself, faith that I will make the right decision. I have to be honest with myself and decide what is best for me.

Chapter 3

Legal Requirements for Marriage

*S*hanice and Ivan had been dating since they were fourteen years old. Both Ivan and Shanice were now sixteen and were talking about getting married.

"We've talked about marriage before," said Ivan. "I love you, and I want to spend the rest of my life with you."

"You know I feel the same way," Shanice replied. "But what about blood tests, a marriage license, and other things like that? I don't even know if we're old enough to be married legally."

"How do we find out about all that stuff?" asked Ivan.

"I don't know," replied Shanice.

In order for a marriage to be recognized by the law, every couple must fulfill certain requirements before they can be married.

Couples who are under a certain age cannot marry without consent from their parents or a judge.

Legal Requirements for a Marriage

Although laws vary from state to state, requirements to get married usually involve a few steps. The couple needs to obtain a license from the state in which they want to get married. There is usually a fee involved for this license.

Many states require the couple to have blood tests done before they can receive a marriage license. The tests will determine if the man or woman has any sexually transmitted diseases (STDs). If one has an STD that the other is not aware of, some states will not issue a license.

Some states require the couple to show proof that they have had all their immunization shots. There are also a few states that require a physical examination.

Most states also require a waiting period of one to five days between the day the license is given and the day of the actual marriage ceremony.

Age Requirements for Marriage

All states require the couple to be of a certain age before they can get married. Most states require teens to be at least eighteen to be married, although this varies from state to state. Couples who fall under the age limit will need permission from their parents to be married. Even with parental consent, most states require that the teens be a certain age.

Couples need to meet certain legal requirements before they can be married.

Most states also allow underage teen couples to get married without parental consent in case of a pregnancy or the birth of a baby. A judge can also give permission for underage teens to marry.

Since laws vary from state to state, it is important to check the laws in your state to see what is required before you can get married. If you get married but do not meet requirements for marriage in your state, the law will not recognize the marriage as legal.

Chapter 4

What Marriage Is All About

When you have an argument with your boyfriend or girlfriend, it is easy to just walk away. You can cool off in your room or by talking to your family. The argument may make you think that this person isn't the right one for you after all.

Once you are married, it's not so easy to walk away or rethink your decision to be with this person. When you made the decision to get married, you made a commitment to spend the rest of your life, for better or worse, with your spouse. It is no longer possible to leave the relationship simply because of an argument. You and your spouse need to work things out. You can't leave a marriage as easily as you can a dating relationship.

Living with Each Other's Habits

We all have habits that can be irritating to others. They may be little things, such as leaving

For some teens, the *idea* of marriage is very glamorous.

dirty dishes in the sink, leaving the toilet seat up, or drinking juice straight from the carton and putting it back in the refrigerator. But these little things can add up to a big thing when you share living space with someone.

Caring about a person can make it more worthwhile to work things out. You can solve little problems before they become big problems. But you must be honest with each other. Gently tell your mate what is bothering you. Admit that you have bad habits yourself. Decide how each of you can change to make the other's life a little easier.

Sharing Chores

Suddenly Mom isn't there to get those 1,095 meals a year on the table. No one puts clean laundry in your drawer. Where is Dad when the sink plugs up or when the storm windows need to be put on? When you are married, all those chores belong to the two of you.

Rick thought doing dishes was women's work. But in Mollie's family, she and her brothers had always shared that chore. She couldn't understand why Rick did not offer to help. When she said something to Rick, he became angry.

When they were both calm and thinking better, Mollie and Rick made a list of chores. Beside each chore they put one or both of their names. From then on things went more smoothly. Sharing the duties and chores is important in any house.

Married But Lonely

After the baby was born, Cheryl stayed home all day. When Doug got back from work at night, she wanted to talk—about anything. But all Doug wanted to do was watch television. He had been talking to people all day. He was tired, and he wanted to be alone.

Everyone needs quiet time. Everyone needs time with others. But you and your mate may need these things at different times. In marriage, you must respect the other person's needs. You must learn to balance "alone" and "together" time to fit each other's needs.

Making Time to Be with Others

Cheryl and Doug talked about their needs. They decided on a plan. On certain afternoons, Cheryl would take the baby out. They would go to see her mother. Or perhaps they would visit one of Cheryl's friends. That way Cheryl got a chance to talk with someone. When Doug got home, the house was quiet. He could have some time alone before Cheryl and the baby got back.

Making special times to see family and friends is a good idea. You and your partner will know when you are expected home. Neither of you will get jealous. And you will look forward to times you will be together.

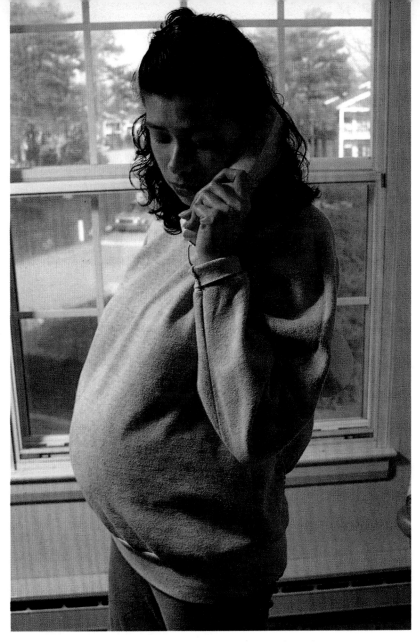

Sometimes marriage is not the cure for loneliness.

Is Marriage 50/50?

Dale and Ann married as teens. They are still happily married, nearly ten years later. Ann says marriage is not a 50/50 deal. "You don't give just half of yourself to a marriage. You give *all* of your-

Careful management of money takes planning and is very important in a marriage.

self and so does your mate. Marriage is 100 percent from both of you."

Others say marriage is more give than take. You give more of yourself. You don't do this to get more in return. You do it because you love the other person and want your marriage to work. Whatever you believe, remember: You don't keep score in marriage. You don't stop giving because the other person doesn't seem to be giving as much.

Chapter 5

Making Ends Meet

The issue of money can become a problem in many marriages. Who will pay for what expenses? Should you pay everything together or split it in half? Do you have enough money to pay the rent and buy food? Money can be an even bigger problem for many married teens.

- *Many married teens drop out of school.* Today, it is very hard to find a good, well-paying job with just a high school diploma. When teens drop out of high school to marry, it becomes even tougher to find a good job to make ends meet.
- *Teens have not had time to learn valuable job skills.* One of the first things employers ask for is job experience. Have you done this job before? Can you run certain kinds of equipment? Teens who have dropped out of high school or even those who have graduated have not had

time to learn or develop the skills needed for
many jobs.
* *Two cannot live as cheaply as one.* When you
  are single, you are the only one spending your
  money. When you are married, there are two of
  you spending. Very often, though, there is *not*
  twice as much money to spend.

Who Will Work?

Toby's mom had never worked outside the
home. Toby wanted his marriage to be like
that, too. But he had trouble paying the bills
on his salary alone. The fact that he could
not support his family made him feel like a
failure.

Manuel didn't feel that way. It was all right
with him if Lisa worked. But Lisa had never
had a job in her life. She wanted to be a home-
maker.

Whichever way you feel, remember this: It is
very hard to support two people on a minimum
wage job. (Minimum wage is the lowest rate of
pay allowed by law.) If only one of you works, that
person will need to make enough money to support both of you. It can be hard to find a job that
pays that much money. You need to have skills,
education, or experience. For some jobs, you need
to have all three. With both of you working, one
doesn't have to be completely dependent on the
other financially.

How Do You Make Ends Meet?

Money is one of the biggest reasons why married couples argue.

"He never puts any money into savings." That's one side of the story.

"There's never anything left *to put into savings."* That's another side of the story.

It can be tough to make ends meet, but there are ways to do it:

- **Make a budget.** List your monthly bills and figure how much money you need to cover them. When you get paid, put that amount of money aside. Use it only to pay those bills.
- **Decide who will pay the bills.** Which one of you is better with money? That person should be in charge of paying the bills, although both of you should know how to do it.
- **What will we do with the extra?** How will you spend money left over after bills and living expenses? (Living expenses are things like food, transportation, personal items, and entertainment.) Will you put it into savings? Will you buy something for your home? Deciding before you get the money often avoids an argument.
- **What will we do if there's not enough?** Again, deciding what you will do *before* this happens avoids arguments. Will you borrow from parents? Will you apply for welfare? Will one of you get another job? If you have a plan, you

don't have to wonder or argue about what you will do.

Where Will You Live?

Many teen couples find that the only place they can afford to rent is not what they had in mind. It may be dirty or too small. It may be in an unsafe neighborhood. It may be too far from family, friends, or work. Deciding where to live is important because your choice of a home can make a big difference in the first year of your marriage.

Chapter 6

A Baby Brings Changes

*S*am and Brenda planned to get married after high school. They were looking forward to being on their own. All their plans changed when Brenda became pregnant.

Suddenly they were married, but it wasn't what they thought it would be. Sam was usually tired and grumpy from going to school during the day and working at night. Brenda was either feeling sick from the pregnancy or worrying about money. She was getting frustrated with everything.

Finally, they decided to go to a social worker for help to work out their problems. The social worker helped them plan for the baby. She gave them advice about how to pay the bills, as well as advice on how to live together happily.

In 1993, more than half a million babies were born to teenage mothers in the United States.

With the addition of a baby, a marriage becomes a family.

More than 200,000 of those babies belonged
to mothers who were under eighteen years of
age. Many of these pregnancies were unplanned.

In this chapter we will talk about how an
unplanned pregnancy can affect a teen couple. We
will look at the options available to teens who are
faced with an unplanned pregnancy.

Pregnancy Means Major Changes

Teens faced with an unplanned pregnancy will
have to make some tough choices about their
future. The pregnancy will create concerns for
both the mother and the father.

Choosing Marriage

Some couples choose to get married because of
a pregnancy. Getting married and having a baby
are two big steps in everyone's life. They bring
major changes. Teens need to prepare themselves
for making some adjustments in their lives. These
teens will have to deal with many issues concern-
ing their future and the future of their baby.
Where will they live? Will they still be able to go
to school? Will they be able to afford the cost of
having a baby? Who will take care of the baby?
How will this baby affect their lives?

How a Baby Will Affect a Marriage

Even if the couple is already married, an unplanned pregnancy can create problems for them.

A baby can create drastic changes in their lives and their marriage. Couples that may have been happily married and enjoying their independence will have to deal with how the baby will change their lives. Their decisions about day-to-day activities, money, and their future will revolve around the baby. Couples need to plan ahead to prepare for these changes.

Other Choices for Pregnant Teens

Marriage isn't the only option available to a couple with a baby on the way. Some couples choose to live together to see how it works before deciding to marry. Others choose not to stay together at all. Single parenting is when either the mother or father raises the child alone. These teens may also have some help from close family and friends. In this situation, the parent not raising the child is required by law to help financially.

Sharing Responsibility

Both the mother and father, whether they are single, married, or divorced, must support their child financially. This support will usually last until the child becomes an adult.

In some cases, a man may deny being the father. In this situation, the mother can sue him for support. If the man is found to be the father, the courts will require him to pay child support. The courts may even require him to pay for the mother's doctor and hospital bills.

If the father refuses to pay, the courts may take a part of his salary and seize his property or bank accounts. In some cases, fathers have even been sent to jail for failing to pay child support.

Abortion and Adoption

Other alternatives to raising a child are abortion or adoption. A couple who chooses to put their child up for adoption gives up their rights as parents. By choosing adoption, the couple decides to sign over their rights for the baby to an agency or to another couple who will raise the child as their own.

Abortion is a medical procedure for stopping pregnancy in its early stages. You need to think carefully and decide whether abortion is the right choice for you.

It may seem like there are too many options to think about. But remember that the only wrong decision is the one that you make in a hurry without all the facts. Making a decision like this is hard; you need to put a lot of thought into it, and be honest with yourself.

It's Your Baby!

Babies bring love into a home. But babies have many needs. They need care and love all the time. They are dependent on their parents for everything.

Being a responsible parent means putting your baby's needs first while finding time for your mate too. If you do not, your marriage will suffer. You must also find time for yourself. If you do not, you will begin to resent your partner and your child.

Marriages can suffer if one's expectations do not come true.

Chapter 7

What If Your Marriage Doesn't Work?

Most of us hope that our marriages will last forever. But today, about half of all marriages end in divorce. For teenagers, this rate is even higher. Only four out of every ten teen marriages last. A girl married at seventeen is *twice* as likely to be divorced as a girl who marries at eighteen or nineteen. If a girl waits until she is twenty-five, the chances that her marriage will last are *four times* better.

Why Does a Marriage Fail?

"With us, it was the little things," said Jim. "We'd argue about stuff like who was going to put gas in the car. Every little thing turned into a big argument. Each time we fought, Julie left. Then one night she didn't come home at all. I knew our marriage was in trouble."

With Carlos and Rita the problem was what *wasn't* said. "We just talked to each other less and less. We spent more time with other people. Pretty soon we just didn't care that much anymore. We should have dated longer. Maybe we would not have gotten married."

How Do You Handle a Problem Marriage?

Shunda knew Perry was a jealous person. But she didn't know *how* jealous until after they were married. "At first he'd just blow up when he saw me talking to another guy. Then one night he beat me. At first I tried to hide it. I wouldn't go out the next day. Finally I went to a women's shelter. It was the best thing I ever did. It's been three years, and we've seen a lot of counselors. Now Perry and I are back together. He doesn't hit me anymore. This time I think it's going to work."

But many times it doesn't work. Shelley and Shawn had been married just six months when Shawn felt they had a problem. "She'd get home later and later from work. I just knew she was seeing someone else. Finally we had it out.

"We agreed not to split until we gave it another try. But a month later, she didn't come home at all one night. I couldn't take it. I left. Maybe I was wrong. But I don't think she ever would have changed."

It is said that time heals everything. This may not always be true, but it is worth a try. Sometimes waiting can save your marriage. Try saying to your mate, "Let's not split up while we're both angry. Let's stay together for a little longer while we try hard to make it work." Give you and your partner a specific period of time and at the end of that time, the answer will usually be clear.

Is Divorce the Only Answer?

Divorce is very painful for both people. It is often just as painful for their families and friends. Children are usually hurt the worst.

Getting a legal separation is another option. It gives you time to think. When you are separated, you do not live with your mate, but you are still married. Spending some time away from each other can be a good thing. It can help you decide what you really want to do.

An annulment is another legal way of ending a marriage. But that must be done soon after the marriage takes place. A couple may realize right away that they have made a big mistake. They have no children. They have not had time to buy things together. So a divorce is not necessary in this particular case.

Where Can I Turn for Help?

If you are thinking about divorce, you are probably feeling very lonely. Talking about your problems can help to solve them. But you may not be able to talk to your mate. Your parents are so upset you don't want to talk with them either. And your best friend doesn't know how to help.

Who else can you talk to? A marriage counselor is trained to listen and help couples with problems. Often a marriage counselor can help you see things clearly. She or he can show you ways to fix your marriage. The counselor will *not* tell you what to do. But he or she *can* help you make up your own mind.

Chapter 8

The Case for Teen Marriage

Today, twenty out of every 100 women getting married for the first time are teens. Out of every 100 men, eight are teens. But many years ago, it was normal for people to marry young. People married younger, and many of those marriages lasted. Divorces were rare.

There are some big differences today. We move and travel a lot. More women work outside the home. There are many more choices and options available to everyone. So it is harder to make a marriage work today—especially a teen marriage. But it *can* be done. Two people who love and respect each other can solve problems together.

Deciding to Make It Work

Joe was sixteen. Emily was seventeen and pregnant. "Everyone—I mean *everyone*—told us not to get married. We were too young. It would never work. But we loved each other and thought we could do it. We made it through having the baby. And after a year we were still together. Then it became a challenge. We wanted to beat the odds, and we have. It hasn't been easy. But you have to work at any marriage. How old you are doesn't matter."

Some Teen Marriages Can Work

Most people at sixteen or seventeen don't know what they want from life. What and who will make them happy for the next seventy years? At seventeen or eighteen, most teens are ready to try life on their own. They may be ready to leave home. But they probably are not ready to choose one partner for the rest of their lives.

Most teens are not ready for marriage. But maybe you are different. Maybe you are very sure about what you want to be. Maybe you *do* know what you want to do with your life. Maybe those goals will not change. Maybe you *are* ready to handle problems like an adult. Some teens are, and they can make their marriages work. But are you *really* one of those few? Or do you just *think* you are?

The only way to tell is to be totally honest. Ask yourself, "Am I *sure* this is what I will want twenty-five years from now? Am I willing to try harder than most people to make it work?" Remember: If you are unsure, you are probably not ready.

Being married and part of a warm, loving family is important for a feeling of well-being.

Being Ready for Change

You may look at life very differently when you're forty or fifty than you do at eighteen or nineteen. You will have many experiences and meet many people in those years. All those things will change your ways of thinking. You must be ready to handle those changes. If you are prepared for them, your marriage can survive.

A Smaller Generation Gap

"Things were different when I was your age." Where have you heard that before? A generation is about thirty years. It is the difference in age between parent and child. But the world can change greatly in thirty years. It is hard for a parent to remember his or her own childhood clearly. This can cause problems between parent and child.

But couples who marry young and have children young decrease this generation gap. When there are only eighteen years between you and your child, life has not changed as much. There are not as many differences between your childhood and your own child's world. You may have a closer relationship with your child because of the smaller difference in age. Also, as a teen, you probably have more energy to give to your child than if you wait until you're older to have kids.

Chapter 9

The Case Against Teen Marriage

Susan was married to Mike when she was sixteen and he was seventeen. They are now divorced. If she could give other teens just one piece of advice on marrying young, it would be, "DON'T DO IT! If you really love each other, it will outlast the wait. There is plenty of time to be married later on. If you are happy with yourself, you will bring so much more into a marriage. It will have a much better chance of lasting."

Why Wait?

Do you have all the same friends now that you did in first grade? At twenty-five, you probably won't have many of the same friends you do at sixteen. The places and people you know and the things you like to do will change greatly in those years.

Marriage brings extra pressures, such as earning money and caring for a home.

A seventeen-year-old girl can cut her chances of divorce *in half* by waiting just one or two more years to marry. You are going to change a lot between your teen years and your mid-twenties. Your friends will change too. The person you wanted to marry at seventeen may be very different from the person you want to be with at twenty-five.

Young Girl/Older Guy

Alex liked having a girl he could protect. He was twenty-two and on his own. Leona was seventeen, insecure, and afraid of the world. Alex took care of everything for her.

Two years later Leona had a high school diploma and a job of her own. She wasn't so insecure anymore. She felt better about herself. She didn't need Alex to protect her. Her life had changed. They separated and soon divorced. Things like this can happen when you or your mate do not have time to grow up before marriage.

What About School?

Pat, married at seventeen, says teen marriage shouldn't happen "unless both of you will stay in school. The people I know who made teen marriages work all went back to finish school."

In a survey done by teacher and author Jean Warren Lindsay, most teens said they would not quit school if they got married. But in the United

States nearly four out of every five teens who get married *do* drop out of school.

Don't Miss the Freedom of Your Teenage Years

The years from eighteen to twenty-five can be wonderful. They can be exciting and full of fun. You finish school. You move out on your own. You get a job and earn your own money. You are young and in good health. You can travel. You have only yourself to take care of. Years later you may say, "I'm so glad I did those things while I could." Never again are you likely to have that freedom.

Is It Worth the Risks?

As a teen, the cards are stacked against you. The odds are not in your favor.

- Your family may be very upset that you want to get married. Your decision may drastically change or end the relationship you have with them. Is it worth the risk?
- The chance of divorce is much higher for teens. Even if you later remarry, that first divorce can leave lasting scars. Is that a chance worth taking?
- What about children? Are you really ready at your age to lead a child through life? Whether or not that child becomes a happy, well-adjusted

adult depends a lot on you. Are you ready for that responsibility?

Only *you* can decide. Take time to make your decisions. Talk with counselors and other adults who will listen with an open mind. Talk with your partner. Have faith in yourself that you can make the right decision.

Chapter 10

Decisions and Your Future

*J*uan and Naomi had only been on a few dates, but everyone was already thinking of them as a couple. Friends began asking them when they were going to get married. They hardly knew each other; how could they be ready for marriage?

Joey and Anna had the opposite problem. They felt that they were ready to get married, but nobody else seemed to agree. Their best friends and families thought it was too soon, and that they were too young. But Joey and Anna had thought about their situation carefully. They had discussed all the things they felt they needed to. They were sure they were ready.

How Do I Know That Something Is Forever?

When you get married, you take a vow, or promise, to be with your mate for life, through good

In the end, only the couple can decide if marriage is the right decision.

times and rough times. So making the decision to get married is a big step, but no one should make this decision except yourself. You must have faith that you are making the right decision.

You need time to think carefully about whether you should get married or not. Ask other people, such as your parents or friends, for help or advice. Think about what changes your decision will bring, and whether you can live with those changes.

Making a decision that is right for you does not mean that you will never have problems. Both you and your spouse will be changing and maturing. Your appearances or personalities may change. Change is normal, but change can affect your marriage and may create problems. You have to think ahead. Are you going to be able to deal with the problems that may come up?

Will I Make the Right Decision?

The decision to marry is probably one of the biggest decisions in a person's life. You will probably be unsure if you made the right decision. But the best way to ensure a good decision is by examining your reasons for getting married.

- Do you love each other?
- Does your relationship have a strong foundation?
- Are you able to work out things together?

- Do you agree on important ideas and respect differences in each other's opinions?

Living Together

Joseph was eighteen and had a full-time job. Marie was seventeen and in her last year of high school. They had been dating for a while and wanted to get married. But they were unsure about how they would get along together sharing living space day and night. Neither of them had ever lived away from home and didn't want to rush into things. After some thought, they decided to move in together as a "trial marriage."

Today, many couples decide to move in together before marrying. These couples may not feel ready to get married. They may not want to jump into something they might regret later. By living together, they will learn to deal with problems that may come up in a day-to-day basis. This will give them a chance to mature and learn to handle things on their own. This will help prepare the couple for the challenges that a marriage can bring.

But not everyone—including teens—agrees with that decision. They feel that if two people truly love each other, there shouldn't be any doubts about the marriage working out.

Still, living together is the decision of the two persons involved. If either one is against it, then it's not the right thing to do. A bad way to start a relationship is by making your mate do something he or she doesn't want to do.

Better with Time

Marriage is a big step for everyone—adults as well as teens. Do not make the decision lightly. It is a decision that will affect the rest of your life. If you don't feel ready to get married, don't let anyone pressure you into it. Remember, just because you say no to your partner when you are seventeen does not mean you will say no when you are twenty-four. The odds that your marriage will work out improve as you get older. Marriage doesn't have to be "now or never." It can be "later."

Marriage is like any relationship—the people involved need to work hard at it in order to make it work. It means a willingness by both partners to support each other, respect the other person's needs and wishes, and compromise when problems come up. These are just some of the criteria necessary for a successful marriage. A successful marriage can bring an enormous sense of joy and accomplishment to any couple.

Glossary—*Explaining New Words*

abortion   A medical procedure that ends a pregnancy in the early stages.

adoption   Process in which the birth parent(s) of a baby or child signs over his or her rights to an agency or to another couple who will raise the child as their own.

commitment   A strong promise or a pledge.

compromise   To settle an argument or difference of opinion with both sides giving up part of what each wants.

divorce   The legal ending of a marriage.

jealousy   Envy; fear of losing someone's love or friendship to another person.

mature   Grown up; acting or thinking like an adult.

minimum wage job   A job that pays the lowest amount of money per hour allowed by the government.

resent   To feel angry or bitter.

responsible   Able to be trusted to do a good job.

sexuality   Ways of looking or acting that emphasize sex.

social worker   A person trained to help people who want to improve their ways of living.

STDs   Sexually transmitted diseases.

tension   Stress; strain; nervousness.

values   Ideals; standards; ways of acting that are important to a person.

vow   A promise.

well-adjusted   Comfortable or pleased with a relationship or way of living.

Where to Go for Help

You can turn to the following people for help or information if you have further questions about teen marriage:

Adults Who Married as Teens
Religious Leaders
School Counselors
Social Workers

You can also contact the following organizations:

Advocates for Youth
1025 Vermont Avenue, NW, Suite 200
Washington, DC 20005
(202) 347-5700

Planned Parenthood Federation of America
810 Seventh Avenue
New York, NY 10019
(212) 541-7800
e-mail: communication@ppfa.org
Web site: http://www.ppfa.org/ppfa/

In Canada
Planned Parenthood Federation of Canada
1 Nicholas Street, Suite 430
Ottawa, Ontario, K1N 7B7
(613) 241-4474

For Further Reading

Berlfein, Judy. *Teen Pregnancy.* San Diego, CA: Lucent Books, 1992.

Bode, Janet, *Kids Having Kids: People Talk About Teen Pregnancy.* New York: Franklin Watts, 1992.

Hughes, Tracey. *Everything You Need to Know About Teen Pregnancy.* New York: The Rosen Publishing Group, Rev. ed. 1997.

Lindsay, Jeanne. *Teenage Couples: Caring, Commitment & Change: How to Build a Relationship That Lasts.* Buena Park, CA: Morning Glory Press, 1996.

Lindsay, Jeanne. *Teenage Couples: Coping with Reality: Dealing with Money, In-Laws, Babies, & Other Details of Daily Life.* Buena Park, CA: Morning Glory Press, 1996.

Trapani, Margi. *Listen Up: Teenage Mothers Speak Out.* New York: The Rosen Publishing Group, 1997.

Index

About the Author
Eleanor Ayer is the author of several books for children and young adults. She holds a master's degree from Syracuse University with a specialty in literacy journalism.

Photo Credits
p. 9 by Maria Moreno; all other photos by Barbara Kirk.